LET'S GO
FISHING
ON THE ICE

GEORGE TRAVIS

The Rourke Corporation, Inc.
Vero Beach, Florida 32964

PHOTO CREDITS
© Wisconsin Department of Tourism: cover, pages 7, 10, 12, 15; © Bob Firth/International Stock: pages 4, 9, 13; © D. Armentrout: page 18; © East Coast Studios: page 6; © Corel: pages 16, 19

FISH ILLUSTRATIONS: © Duane Raver

PROJECT EDITOR: Duane Raver
Duane Raver received a degree in Zoology with a major in fishery management from Iowa State University. Employed by the North Carolina Wildlife Resources Commission as a fishery biologist in 1950, he transferred to the Education Division in 1960. He wrote and illustrated for the magazine *Wildlife in North Carolina*. Mr. Raver retired as the editor in 1979 and is a freelance writer and illustrator.

EDITORIAL SERVICES: Penworthy Learning Systems

Library of Congress Cataloging-in-Publication Data

Travis, George. 1961-
   Let's go fishing on the ice / by George Travis.
      p. cm. — (Let's go fishing)
   Includes index
   Summary: Describes some of the techniques used to catch fish in frozen lakes.
   ISBN 0-86593-464-9
   1. Ice fishing—Juvenile literature. [1. Ice fishing.]
2. Fishing.] I. Title. II. Series: Travis, George, 1961
Let's go fishing.
SH455.45.T735 1998
799.1'22—dc21   97–49077
                                       CIP
                                       AC

Printed in the USA

TABLE OF CONTENTS

WHAT IS ICE FISHING?

Fishing through a hole cut in ice is called ice fishing. During the winter, lakes freeze and become good places to ice fish.

The water gets colder as winter comes. After the surface temperature drops below 32° F (0° C), the lake freezes. The ice floats on top.

The deeper water stays the warmest. The fish usually stay in the deeper water. That is where they find enough oxygen to survive.

The ice on this frozen lake is thick enough to walk on!

CHOOSING THE RIGHT SPOT

Four inches (about 10 centimeters) of ice is safe to walk on. Do not walk on the ice if you can see cracks or seams.

If you are not sure how thick the ice is, have an experienced angler check for you.

The ice must be 4 or more inches thick to be safe to walk on.

If the ice is thick enough, many people can fish at the same time.

To find fish, get on your knees and look through the ice. If the lake is free of snow, you should be able to see down into the water. Look for places where fish gather, such as weedbeds, dropoffs, rocks, or sunken logs.

CUTTING THE HOLE

When you have found a spot, you can begin to cut the hole. There are a few different tools for this job. Drilling a hole by using a spoon or screw **auger** (AW ger) is one way. A **spud** (SPUD) is the simplest tool to use. It is a heavy bar that has a sharp, flat end.

Use the spud to chip the ice away. The hole should be at least eight inches (over 20 centimeters) wide. You can use the spud to smooth the bottom edge of the hole. Smoothing prevents the sharp ice from cutting your fishing line.

This man is using a screw auger to cut a hole in the ice.

ICE FISHING EQUIPMENT

People who ice fish use basic equipment. An ice fishing rod is shorter than other rods. It allows you to sit closer to the hole and see what is happening.

You can use a thermometer to find the warm areas in the water where the most fish are. An empty five-gallon bucket is good for carrying your fishing gear and the fish you catch. It also makes a good seat while you fish. You can scoop out the ice shavings and keep the hole open with a strainer.

It is warmer to sit on a bucket than on the ice and snow.

THE PERFECT BAIT

Different **bait** (BAYT) is used to catch different fish. Minnows are the most-used live bait. Crappie, pike, bass, trout, perch and walleye all feed on live minnows.

Most fish will feed on earthworms, another common live bait. Even brown trout—picky eaters, especially in winter—like earthworms.

Keeping your catch on ice stops them from spoiling.

This father teaches his son how to bait a hook.

Artificial (AHR tuh FISH ul) bait is also used for catching trout and perch.

Sunny days with no snow on top of the ice will affect the feeding of fish. Sunlight helps plants produce oxygen in the water, and the fish may feed more. Some fish, such as yellow perch, crappies, and walleyes, feed when the sun goes down.

JIGGING

Jigging (JIG ging) is a type of fishing by jerking a line up and down in the water. A jigstick is a short stick with a special shaped handle. The fishing line winds around the jigstick.

When jigging you can use **natural** (NACH ur ul) or artificial bait. One artificial bait is a jig. It is usually small with a heavy, metal head and often has feathers or fur tied around the hook.

Jigging is a good way to attract and catch fish both large and small. A row of holes lets you move easily to where the fish are feeding.

A short rod allows this man to sit close to the hole.

TILT OR TIP-UP

Tilt or **tip-up** (TIP up) is another way to ice fish. A tip-up is a spring with a line tied to it, along with a hook and bait.

Once a fish bites, the line is pulled, the spring releases, the hook is jerked, and a flag comes up. Now the **angler** (ANG gler) knows a fish has hit the bait on that line.

Anglers use the tip-up to catch larger fish. You can set up more than one tip-up at a time. Be sure to check local fishing rules, though.

Anglers often set up many tip-ups at a time.

PROTECTING YOURSELF

Proper clothing is important when ice fishing. Layers of loose-fitting clothes help keep you warm. Gloves are important for protecting your hands and fingers. Bring an extra pair in case one gets wet.

Warm, waterproof clothing must be worn if you go ice fishing.

Ice shanties are used for shelter from the cold weather.

Good boots and heavy socks help keep your feet warm and dry. A knitted cap is good to protect your ears.

Some ice fishermen build a little house called an ice **shanty** (SHAN tee). The shanty is then placed over the hole in the ice. You can sit inside for protection from the cold wind.

SAFETY FIRST

Always check the ice before going on it. If it is less than four inches (10 centimeters) thick, do not try to ice fish.

Look for dark spots on the ice, especially in early and late winter. The spots may be weak areas in the ice.

Never, never ice fish alone. If you should fall through the ice, no one would know it.

fish: Arctic char *(Salvelinus alpinus)*
average weight: 8 lbs.
(3.6 kilograms)
location: Alaska, northern
Canada and New England, Greenland, Iceland

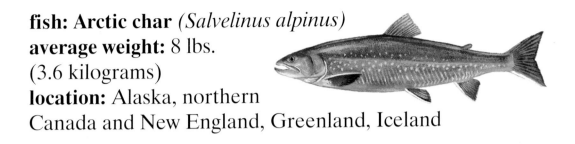

---

fish: bluegill *(Lepomis macrochirus)*
average weight: 8 ozs. to 1 lb.
(113 grams to .45 kilograms),
may reach over 4 lbs.
(1.8 kilograms)
location: from the Great Lakes
to the Gulf and New Mexico

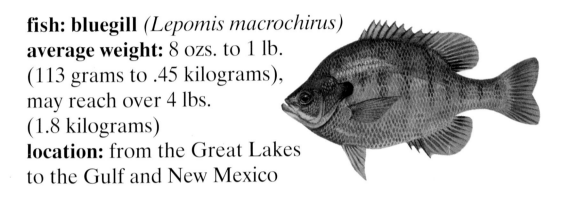

---

fish: brown bullhead *(Ameiurus nebulosus)*
average weight: 1 to 3 lbs (.45 kilograms
to 1.36 kilograms)
location: the Great Lakes
and Maine south to Mexico
and Florida

---

fish: brown trout *(Salmo trutta)*
average weight: 1 to 3 lbs. (.45 kilograms
to 1.36 kilograms)
location: Norway to North
Africa and Ireland to Russia,
North and South America, Australia, New Zealand,
Africa, and India

fish: chain pickerel *(Esox niger)*
average weight: 2 lbs.
(.9 kilograms), may reach
9 lbs., 6 oz. (4.3 kilograms)
location: Atlantic drainages from Nova Scotia to Florida,
Mississippi basin from Missouri south

---

fish: northern pike *(Esox lucius)*
average weight: 10 to 20 lbs.
(4.5 to 9.1 kilograms),
may reach 75 lbs.
(34 kilograms)
location: northern Europe, Labrador west to Alaska,
south to Pennsylvania, Missouri and Nebraska

---

fish: walleye *(Stizostedion vitreum)*
average weight: 3 lbs.
(1.4 kilograms), may reach
25 lbs. (11.3 kilograms)
location: Northwest Territories east
to Québec, southeast to Alabama

---

fish: yellow perch *(Perca flavescens)*
average weight: may reach 4 to
5 lbs. (1.8 to 2.7 kilograms)
location: from the Northwest
Territories to as far south as
South Carolina

GLOSSARY

angler (ANG gler) — person who fishes

artificial (AHR tuh FISH ul) — made by human beings rather than nature

auger (AW ger) — a hole driller

bait (BAYT) — something, usually food, placed on a hook to attract fish

jigging (JIG ging) — a method of fishing by jerking a line up and down in the water

natural (NACH ur ul) — produced by or found in nature

shanty (SHAN tee) — a little house put over a hole in the ice for protection from the cold and wind

spud (SPUD) — a heavy bar with a flat end used to cut a hole in the ice

tip-up (TIP up) — a method of fishing using a spring, hook, bait, and flag

INDEX

FURTHER READING:

Find out more about fishing with these helpful books and information sites:
Griffen, Steven A., *The Fishing Sourcebook: Your One-Stop Resource for Everything You Need to Feed Your Fishing Habit.* The Globe Pequot Press, 1996
Gruenwald, Tom. *Hooked on Ice Fishing.* Krause Publications, 1995
Waszczuk, Henry and Labignan, Halto. *Freshwater Fishing. 1000 Tips from the Pros.* Key Porter Books, 1993
Fishernet online at www.thefishernet.com
National Marine Fisheries Service online at www.nmfs.gov
World of Fishing online at www.fishingworld.com